WOW Your Customers!

7 Ways to World-Class Service

John D. Hanson

Table of Contents

The **7 Ways** Advantage

Are you looking for fresh ideas to achieve world-class customer service in an approach that is customized just for you? **7 Ways** has the solution! As an added bonus, this is the only resource on the market that literally pays you back as you share it with others........with no limits on how much we will thank you! Let me share with you how this guide can transform your customers' experiences, pay for itself, and more! Here's how it works:

- ✓ Go to our secure website: www.7waysmenu.com
- ✓ Register for free to receive your unique promo code
- ✓ Share your promo code to give others a double **Bonus**
- ✓ You receive a **Thank You Bonus** every time your promo code is used
- ✓ Your **Thank You Bonuses** add up to earn **unlimited** $20 Amazon eGift cards!
- ✓ Receive a **Thank You Bonus** per person for all registered **7 Ways in 77 Minutes** Workshops
- ✓ Get a **Bonus** for every future **7 Ways** purchase!

According to a 2013 study by Columbia University, the average American knows between 300-600 people. It only takes 25 referrals to earn your first Amazon eGift card! So register today!!

7 Ways in 77 Minutes Workshops

7 Ways in 77 Minutes Workshops are time-conscious training events ideal for businesses or small groups. Included in the package is a copy of *WOW Your Customers! 7 Ways to World-Class Service* for each attendee along with a personal tutorial and Q&A session. As an added bonus, the one who organizes the event can register on our secure website, www.7waysmenu.com, and receive the **Thank You Bonus** for every attendee enrolled! Best of all, your team receives the book for less than the list price! So register today!!

Acknowledgements

There have been so many people who have contributed to my art of skillful customer service: Tim in retail; Bob in insurance and sales; Richard, Robert, Matt & Matthew in faith-based non-profit; Linda & Jim in warehousing; Mitch, Brandi, Valerie, Penny, and Mary in finance; Zoreda, Fred, Tammy, Romeo and Heath in credit services; Mark and Josh in logistics, Gary and Julie in manufacturing; and Todd, Tim, Jim, Mary and a host of others in industrial automation.

My deep appreciation to the recommendation and mentoring of Brian Tracy. Since my first seminar in 2000, Brian's win/win, compassionate approach to serving others, whether it be in sales, leadership or customer service, has been invaluable. His sincere endorsement required time out of his very full schedule; I am extremely honored and grateful.

Thank you very much, Eric, for the many hours of creative support and responsive updates. The book and website would have been impossible without your cheerful, artistic contributions!

The **7 Ways in 77 Minutes** Workshop would not have been possible without your artistic input, Karly! Your creative abilities saved me valuable hours to craft content and resulted in an attractive, concise presentation.

Thank you, Robert, for the in-depth editorial contribution! How grateful I am for one of my dearest college professors to be an integral part of this book.

My wife has been unshakable in her faithful support and loving accountability. Without her love through all the tough times, I would not be the person I am today. Our children possess creative, teachable spirits that bless me every day to be their father; their great patience during the lean times has been an inspiration to me.

The greatest credit for any success I experience belongs to my heavenly Father, for it is His favor and kindness to me that blesses me with the very breath of life. Every day is a fresh opportunity to do my very best for His glory.

Recommendations

My humble thanks to those who sent their thoughtful, sincere feedback. The full collection of all feedback can be found on our website under the heading: "What People Are Saying."

"This powerful, practical book is loaded with ideas and insights to generate 'customers for life.'"

**Brian Tracy, Author, *Maximum Achievement,*
www.briantracy.com**

"John embodies a rare combination of capabilities and personality traits that are too often separated from each other. He is highly skilled and an eminent professional... while still being authentic and approachable. It is a pleasure to do business with someone that not only moves a project forward with understanding and competence, but who makes the process enjoyable and is a true pleasure to work with. Truly a gifted, humble professional that is a delight to work with."

Luke Milton, Creative Director, Vision House Studio,

VisionHouse.pro

"John has always given our company top notch service. Whenever we reached out for help or information on a particular issue, he was always there, ready to round up the expertise needed for the task. There was never that pushiness you get with some salesman. It was always just the facts and a personable, sincere touch that can only come from putting customers first and meaning it. Best of luck on the book, and I can't wait to read it!"

Paul G., System Admin., Automotive Mfg., 25 years

"I appreciate the work John does for us. He always asks questions and works to understand my needs for every situation. He treats every interaction we have as an important one and gives them a high level of attention & responsiveness. He always takes the extra step to make sure questions are answered, quotes or orders are completed & submitted, and issues are taken care of completely to everyone's satisfaction. Thanks for all you do, John!"

Ian Visintine, Proj. Eng., Martin Control Systems, Inc., www.martincsi.com

"John is my go-to man in the situations where improvement is needed and I'm at a loss for that final component for success...I recommend John as an Account Manager as he cares for you and your company's success."

Gary Evans, Automation Mgr., Corvac Composites, Greenfield, OH

"John D. Hanson is an excellent account manager, in that he is able to discern his customer's real issues, break them down into smaller manageable problems, and provide sound solutions. His ability to concisely convey this information to me, makes my job as the vendor support a lot easier, and ultimately, provide the best solution for the customer. I look forward to working on projects with John and his customers."

Oliver Lizotte, Applications Engineer, Piab NA, Hingham, MA

"John has provided excellent customer service to our facility. Anytime we have had questions about what products would provide us the best solution for our processing issues, he not only coordinated all of the product specialists for that equipment, he also set up several technical on-site demonstrations for our process engineers. Every correspondence with him has been extremely professional, and his response time is amazing. If you looked up World-Class Customer Service on the internet, I would anticipate John D. Hanson's photo would pop up immediately!"

Janice Litz, Sr. Quality Engineer, Whirlpool, Marion, OH

"John D. Hanson takes 5-star customer service and professionalism to the next level. He puts the customer's needs first and will go the extra mile to make sure the customer experience is as smooth as possible. I am always happy to go on joint sales calls with John as he projects professionalism while handling business needs and managing the relationships that have been, and continue to be, established in the industrial automation world."

Frank Raburn, Sales Development, Pizzato, New Hudson, MI

"John met with me on a few sales calls that he thought our company would be a good resource to provide his client with the right solution. John has always provided prompt communication and feedback to his clients. He keeps a professional attitude in every situation he is in. Creating relationships with clients can sometimes be difficult and somehow John seems to always make it look easy. John's excitement and enthusiasm for providing the best Customer Service possible is very contagious."

Jason Angle, Bus. Development Mgr., Force Design, Inc., forcedesign.biz

"John has always been very professional, looking at the whole picture for most situations. This process has assisted him in making very calculated and accurate decisions. The ability to quickly make those calculated decisions attributed to building trust and positive rapport which carries an enormous amount of weight, especially in customer service."

Isaac Nuss, Air Defense Artillery Officer, Ohio Army National Guard

"In my time working with John Hanson, he has exhibited above average professionalism. His work ethic exceeds our company's exceptional standards, and his customer service skills go above and beyond what is expected. John is very knowledgeable on our product lines and is always willing to learn more in areas he may be lacking in order to be the best account manager he can be for our customers. Aside from his job performance on a technical level, John is one of the kindest, most respectful people I have ever had the pleasure of working with. He is a huge asset to our company and I am proud to work along-side him."

Erica Adams, Accounting Support Specialist,
Voelker Controls Company

"I have been in the world of manufacturing for over 28 years, and the number one aspect of success I was taught early on was as follows: Be a good listener! If you don't listen to the customer, then no matter how good a communicator you are, you will not be viewed as a true solutions provider. Too often, we go into sales calls or meetings, and we have already set out in our minds what we want to accomplish. When doing this, too many times it is hard to adjust on the fly and react according to the customers' responses/needs. With that said, let me describe John with a brief statement...If I could clone John and place more John's throughout my territory, my job would be simplified tenfold! In today's fast-paced world of business, if you don't have the proper professionalism or skills of listening, then you will be left behind. John not only has these attributes but he performs them with ease. It is a true pleasure to work with someone like John, and I look forward to doing so for many years to come."

Jason Angelicchio, Area Sales Mgr.-Great Lakes, Piab NA

Introduction

Why You Won't Be Able to Put This Book Down!

World-class customer service is highly-valued in today's competitive, global marketplace. Yet it is so hard to find! Whether you are a sole proprietor or a Fortune 500 team member, there is a need for fresh, straightforward ideas to revitalize customer service efforts. Consider the following questions:

- Are you working to improve your customer service feedback?
- Are you satisfied with your customer and employee retention?
- Are you adding and keeping strong performers on your team?
- Do you want to boost your profits AND customer satisfaction?
- Do you want to add more engaged, loyal customers?
- Are you searching for cost-effective training with no inventory in just one session?

The **7 Ways** approach can simply address these concerns while revitalizing your customer service at the same time! Here are 7 **Ways** you will benefit from reading this book:

- Revolutionize the concept of winning
- Unlock simple secrets to greater productivity
- Create proactive, positive communication
- Forge strong, long-lasting interpersonal bonds
- Brighten others' days as an energy giver
- Connect with customers on a deep, personal level
- Exceed your customers' expectations

Best of all, the **7 Ways** approach is based on: "It's a menu, not a recipe!" Take what works best for you and add it to your processes. There is always more than one way to take the best care of our customers; make these **7 Ways** work for you! I encourage you to take notes; if you're a note-taker, make personalized marks throughout the book. And at the end of every chapter, I've included space to write your very own recipe. Jot down the "ingredients" from each chapter that connected with you!

Before we dive into **What** the 7 Ways approach is, let me share with you **Why** I created this book and workshop. Ever since I was a child, how people feel has been important to me. In conversations, as others talk, I observe the body language, expressions, tone and words of the ones in the conversation. I feel badly for those who are misunderstood, not heard, ignored, patronized or confused. So I have resolved to be careful with my words, my tone, my body language, and how I treat others; I work to put myself in others' shoes. My commitment to empathetic encouragement should result in being a blessing to those around me. While it may seem like I'm trying to be liked by everyone, my goal is to never be offensive or hurtful to anyone, as much as possible.

As my career path has progressed, this personal priority has repeatedly brought leadership opportunities, increased responsibilities and, most importantly, team members and customers who enjoy working with me. In diverse fields like non-profit, retail, hospitality, finance, logistics, industrial automation, warehousing, and the military, my superiors and my peers have recognized my ability to work well with others. In the companies that measure customer satisfaction, I consistently scored in the highest rating level, earning top CSAT scores consistently at two different companies.

At the beginning of 2017, I committed to a personal goal of regularly reading books before bedtime. My purposes were to engage my mind, limit digital screen time, add value to my personal relationships and achieve my business goals. During that reading time, I was struck with how critical it is to provide excellent customer service in order to earn long-term, win-win successes. That's when I had "the light bulb moment."

What if I could share the core principles I used successfully in every career step so that team members, leaders and business owners could experience the same success? What if customer service agents in front-line roles could discover how incredibly freeing excellent customer service can be? What if a small business up to a Fortune 500 company could revolutionize their customer service experiences through a simple, cost-effective process that added personal and professional value to their teams? These ideas were the starting points for the 7 **Ways** approach to life and business.

Stellar customer service does not come naturally, and it is not easy to do. It takes commitment, practice and genuine empathy to hone the skills needed to provide industry-leading customer service.

No matter what the title is on our business card,

we are all in the business of providing service to our customers. Consistently striving for exceptional customer service is the lifeblood of our business,

for without customers, we have no business.

But why is this book important for you or your team to read? No matter what the title is on our business card, we are all in the business of providing service to our customers. Consistently striving for exceptional customer service is the lifeblood of our business, for without customers, we have no business. The individuals, leaders and businesses that make excellent customer service a top priority will experience a growing amount of long-term, win-win successes. The companies that model, teach and reward engaging customer service will retain the employees who are skilled at it and will foster a strong, positive work environment.

By studying industry-leading companies like Amazon, American Express, Disney, Nordstrom and Ritz-Carlton, I discovered how invaluable such service is to attracting and retaining loyal, long-term customers and team members. You will benefit immensely from what I've learned. With an exhausting number of involved ways to improve customer service available, the **7 Ways** approach is designed to provide a simple, easily-repeatable, individualized process. Jim Collins, in *Good to Great*, validates the value of this formula for success. He confirmed that providing people with a few messages constantly works far better than introducing new ones every month or quarter. **7 Ways** is more about a fresh mindset rather than a whole new method, equipping team members rather than educating them.

Let me share the **7 Ways** our workshop can add value to you:

- Very affordable! Earn a significant discount off the book's list price for every attendee
- Customizable **7 Ways** Menu for each attendee
- Self-managed by your team
- Measure the impact on your team with your current analytic tools
- No scripts
- No inventory
- Simply schedule a **7 Ways in 77 Minutes** Workshop for your new team members in the future!

With a minimal investment of just 77 minutes, **7 Ways** adds a proven, simple approach to revitalize your customer service efforts. It's easy to learn, easy to use and easy to manage!

Like a bright-red cherry perched on top of your sundae, let's add a tangible financial benefit. In 2010, a customer service survey found that 85% of customers would spend 5-25% more to ensure a superior customer service experience. That was during the post-2008 recession; imagine the impact now in the social media era for providing exceptional customer service! Not only is providing first-class service the right thing to do, it is still a proven investment into earning long-term, win-win successes---lots and lots of successes! So I look forward to sharing with you **7 Ways** that are invaluable in taking the best care of every customer you serve. These proven principles have not cost me a dime; they do require consistent commitment in time and effort with a genuine concern for the customers' best interests. The business successes and recognition for me were added bonuses to the deep, personal satisfaction of being an invaluable asset to my customers and to my team. Connect your motivated professionals with these steps, and your organization will experience dramatic improvements in customer loyalty and satisfaction. So will your bottom line!

Winning

"Winning isn't always championships."

---Michael Jordan

Before we begin exploring these **7 Ways** together, I want to encourage you to look at it like this: "It's a menu, not a recipe!" Just like a drink and a main course make a meal, there are two of the **7 Ways** that I believe are critically important to have. The other five--try them, see if you like them, and add them to your processes when there is value for you.

What it is

One of the most incredible paradigm shifts I had in my personal reading, was the definition of winning. Oftentimes, we know what a word means--or we *think* we know what a word means--either by what we've been told by others or what we have thought for so long ourselves. But what does the word "winning" actually mean? So I went to the dictionary. Exciting stuff, I know!

The first definition made perfect sense--coming in first or excelling in competition – what I expected. But it was the second definition that really changed my entire perspective on winning. Do you know the second definition of winning?

Success. **Success is winning.** To put it more clearly, the vast majority of people in the world are already winners, and they don't even realize it. If our definition of winning is based on the results of others or the hard work of others, then our success will always be dependent upon what someone else does! Mind blown!!

Success IS Winning!

When I realized this, it made me think of famous athletes that we all know. I doubt that they've won every single competition they have entered. Yet they are labeled as winners. Why is that? It's their mindset--their approach to their sport, their drive to continuously improve, to get consistently better. They realize that the day-in, day-out effort directly contributes to their success.

So if you're reading this book to improve your customer service, you're already a winner! The fact is that the vast majority of what we do in a day is successful. So the more appropriate question is: do you want to win more? Do you want to succeed more? I believe we do! Keep this frame of reference in mind as you go forward in this book. It will be absolutely critical to get the most out of these **7 Ways**. As a matter fact, this whole new concept of what winning actually is, that's going to be a book by itself. But that's for another time!

Why

After we re-define what winning is, it's important to understand the purpose behind what we do – the **Why**.

Simon Sinek has excellent material on LinkedIn and YouTube called *Start with the Why*. I highly recommend reviewing some of these videos, as they have been very insightful for me.

When you start with the **Why**, age is not most important, neither is experience. What's most important is that everybody is on the same page in an organization. When we have an understanding of **Why** we are doing what we do, it is far easier to be motivated to do well.

Think back to the first time you were introduced to the most attractive opportunity of your career. Remember the excitement and nerves facing that first interview---learning about the company, about your coworkers, about the leadership. It was all new and fresh to you. Then think about how excited you were to receive an offer to work at that place where you really connected with their vision—you couldn't wait to start! Because we want to add value to the place where we work, one of the important **Why**'s is respect for those we work for and those we work alongside--adding value to the organization. It's a business owner mindset—"If I was the owner, how would I want my team to perform?" I look at it the same way, as if it's my business; I want to run it well.

Another key **Why** is to take care of our customers. No matter what the title is on our business card, it is essential that we provide excellent customer service to everyone. **Customers are the lifeblood of our business, for without customers, we have no business.** The quality of our products and/or services should make price a secondary consideration. When our customers know they're supported by people who care, they'll think of us first.

Be responsive *and* accurate

Along with being friendly and personable, it is just as important that we be accurate. After all, a fast answer that's incorrect creates more work for us and our customer than a correct answer given a little bit more slowly. So even in our global, fast-paced world, it is very important to make sure that we're being **responsive *and* accurate**. The long-term success of our organization depends on the quality of our service. Invested team members understand the **Why** of what we do and respond with excellent care. Customers notice!

To give you an example of how important the motivation behind excellent customer service is, consider the graph on the next page. A recent customer service survey showed that 80% of businesses provided average or below customer service. Only 10% provided above average customer service, and only 5% provided world-class customer service. To put that into perspective, the vast majority of companies are providing exactly what people are expecting...or worse. Engaged employees make an enormous difference in the level of service customers receive, and industry leaders in customer service are chock full of engaged, enthusiastic team members.

Understanding the **Why** of what they do is one reason why these companies consistently win.

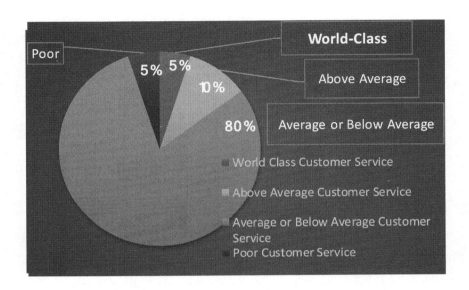

Who

Another aspect of winning that can help with motivation behind what we do, is to understand **Who** is important to us. **Our families and loved ones** are the strongest emotional motivator for us to win more. Here is the perfect example.

How many of you have experienced either job loss or underemployment? During those tight financial times, do you recall the countless hours spent applying for and interviewing for better opportunities, only to hear: "Your interview was great! Unfortunately, we've decided to go with someone else." On top of this, did it seem like one major item after another in your home or on your vehicle decided to call it quits? And no matter how hard you tried to catch back up, you fell further and further behind financially?

**There is no stronger motivation
on the face of the earth
than taking care of our loved ones**

If this sounds familiar, you're not alone; it happened to us a few years ago. During that time, I was working two jobs and going to school online full-time. My story is not unique to our family; so many people work through demanding times in their lives like this. Why? For **Who**? Their loved ones and their futures. There is no stronger motivation on the face of the earth than taking care of the loved ones in our lives.

Throughout my career, I have been blessed to work with many professional, personable leaders who gave of themselves to improve my service. Several of these relationships were in industries that I had no previous experience. These leaders were adding me, an unknown to their team, and I made the most of it!

Be a mentor, not a manager

Think of the leaders who hired you into a great opportunity. How excited were you to start work on your first Monday? How motivated were you to learn as much as you could about the company, the customers, the team and the opportunity? It was the same anticipation for me. My gratitude for their trust in me inspired me to work even harder to make them and their team a success. And my attitude at work positively influenced my team members. When my team asked how I liked my job, I would always say how grateful I was to work for our leader. We had all worked for managers (a role) and mentors (a relationship). The first role was a title—manager: often supported by their authority to get the work done. The second role was a trust—mentor: as they worked alongside and served the customers & the team, the work was completed with less effort and greater quality.

If you are currently working with a good leader, with a mentor, thank them! These influencers do not grow on trees! **Great leaders** are a **Who** in our approach to **Winning**, and their impact can change a life!

Let me share a story from the most difficult time of my life—military basic training. Not only did I train in Georgia in the hot summer months (I remember praying for just a little breeze, any breeze!), but I also learned that many high school juniors would train in the summer months before returning to complete the second half of their training after their senior year. My enlistment with the Army National Guard began when I was 32 years old. To say that the difference in maturity, patience and teamwork was different between a 17-year-old and a 32-year-old, is an enormous understatement! I learned patience the hard way...with a lot of exercise...and not by choice! The younger soldiers had a more difficult time learning to think about the team first. It is absolutely essential that soldiers learned to shift from a focus on themselves as individuals to the unit as a whole. In order for the unit to be more effective in battle, we all had to understand that it was important to stop thinking about **Me**, and start thinking about **We**.

We versus Me

Another definition from Webster's dictionary that I really appreciate is the word **synergy**: increased effectiveness that results when two or more people or businesses work together. Energy will only take you so far; synergy will combine energies and result in far greater achievements.

"Good enough" is the enemy of "Great!"

I vividly remember my first interview for my current responsibility in the fascinating world of industrial automation. I asked the owner what were some of the key principles he saw in his top performers within the company. The most important approach he said was, "Don't be a Lone Ranger. Involve others in your efforts. Include the specialists who have far more experience in your activities. When you're engaging with customers, you will add more value to them, more effectively identify their issues, and propose more valid solutions." That advice has served me very well! In the realm of customer service, it is even more important to have a strong team working towards world-class customer service.

Obviously, **our customers** are the most critically-important **Who** to us. The greatest threat to providing excellent customer service is what I call "good enough." If the effort that we're putting into something is "Good enough", that's exactly what most people experience—remember, they're constantly experiencing average or below-average customer service. "Good enough" is the enemy of "Great!"

So we want to take either dissatisfied or barely-satisfied customers and change them into engaged, loyal customers. The difference is gigantic! When I worked for Chase in their mortgage re-finance department, we had a professional attorney who was one of our valued clients. During one of her refinances, the process did not go as smoothly for her as they had in the past. Her conversations with the loan processor, in the desk directly across from me, often escalated into a shouting match over the phone! So my manager came to me and said, "John, would you be willing to take this over for us?" I jumped at the opportunity! I love the challenge of converting unsatisfied customers into loyal, engaged promoters.

Through constant communication, keeping her updated, diligently working through the tasks that needed to get done, and meeting deadlines, we were able to complete the refinance for her and, more importantly, keep her business with us. Not only did she ask for me to process her future refinances, she was the only customer of the hundreds of people I served that sent me a Christmas card. That meant so much to me! I had made that much of a difference in her life! She took time out of her busy day to send a personally-signed Christmas card to one processor at our huge corporate office with thousands of employees. That's the difference between a satisfied and an engaged customer!

They think of us first because the relationship is far more important than the price. They can always find a better price somewhere else, but they are not guaranteed of the service they will receive. Because our service has already been proven, they become eager advocates for us. It's a proven fact – engaged customers spend more. How much more? A recent Gallup study showed that engaged customers spent 22 to 56% more! So to put that into perspective, just for an example, say your sales are $1 million a year. By transforming satisfied customers into loyal engaged ones, your sales could jump from $1 million all the way up to $1.5 million. That's a huge difference!

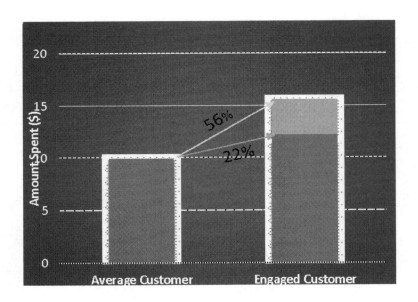

Keeping a loyal, engaged customer is far cheaper in time and money then winning a new one! The Harvard Business Review states that it costs from 5% to 25% more to win new customers. On top of this, if customers are kept just 5% more, revenue increases by 25 to 95%! By engaging your existing customers, you can transform them from satisfied to loyal promoters. In the last chapter, I will share with you **7 Ways** to engage your customers. It is good for them **and** good for you!

When

Have you ever heard someone say, "I would love to have that car!" How do you know if that's a wish or a goal? Here's how. Do they know the exterior color? Do they know the engine type? Do they know the wheels they want? Do they know the interior material? Do they know when they're going to buy it? If a person doesn't know the answer to these simple questions, then it's a wish, not a goal. Suppose they know all these details, and it is a goal. Would you like to know how to achieve it faster?

Write it down. And when you do write it down, make sure that it's very specific. Along with writing goals down, it's very important that we see them every day. So whether it's on paper or on a digital screen, we need to keep them in front of us. This engages both our conscious and subconscious mind to achieve our goals.

Be What You See!

Be What You See!

A Dominican University study showed there was a significant difference in achieving goals when they were written down versus just being in the mind only. Here's why.

- It creates a vision

- Progress can be measured

- Benchmarks can be set as key steps along the way

- When the end goal is achieved, party!!!

How can you celebrate if you don't know when you've arrived? Along the way, keep track of any and all progress. Remember that a step in the right direction is a step closer to your end goal. If you feel stuck, discuss your concerns with a mentor, a manager or a coworker you trust. By the way, that Dominican University study proved that **written goals** are achieved 30% more than just mental goals. So write them down!

Of all the **7 Ways**, **Winning** (or how to win more, to be precise) is **the most important tool** you can add to your customer service toolbox. Always remember that you are already winning. Determine to pursue winning even more!

Your **W**inning Order

_____

_____

_____

_____

_____

_____

_____

Let's Get Organized!

"A good system shortens the road to the goal."

Ralph Waldo Emerson

Now be honest with me, when you saw this chapter heading, did you think to yourself, "Oh crap! We're going to talk about being organized?!" Before you skip this chapter though, please hear me out! This is not intended to change who you are, your style or your personality. This is just another tool, another item on the menu, that I'd like you to consider. Oh, and it's proven to help you be more productive with less stress...well worth taking a look!

Who comes to your mind when organization is mentioned? Someone with OCD or perfectionists that are always straightening pictures (that's me!) or neat freaks? How about analytical nerds with slide rules in their pockets and half an office supply store?! Or people that are all about the process-- getting the process better—who often overlook the people in the process?

Less clutter equals less stress

No matter who comes to our minds, the benefits of organization are proven to improve health, productivity and relationships. This is based off the simple fact that less clutter equals less stress. And lower stress improves not only health and productivity, but mood, focus and attitude as well. Our stress level has a subconscious impact on us that is far stronger than we realize. So let's explore some ways to improve organization both personally and professionally.

When I was a soldier in the Ohio Army National Guard, I had the privilege to work with one of the most professional supply sergeants in the entire battalion. He was responsible for items that were decades old and likely to never be used again. But each item had to be accounted for, as he was responsible to the taxpayers to keep track of every single item our tax dollars bought. Even though the sergeant's strongest personality trait was not that of an organizer, he was so professional that he meticulously accounted for the items both in written **and** picture form. He set the standard in the battalion for how to track every item in inventory the best way possible. It does not require this to be a natural personal strength for you to benefit yourself and your organization.

Keep ahead

One of the best ways to become more organized is simple--- start early. Let's call it the "AM Advantage". When I worked for Chase with thousands of employees, the benefits were easily seen. Better parking spaces, lighter traffic, getting hours of productivity in before the busiest part of the day – these all enabled better productivity with less work and lower stress. The cumulative advantage of gained productivity over the course of a year was immense!

One of the best ways to become more organized; start early!

As a senior loan processor for Chase, I started in the summer of 2012, right in the middle of the refinance boom. Mortgage interest rates were in the 3% range, and demand was at an all-time high. Because of high turnover, caseloads went from an average of 60 per processor to close to 100 files! Unlimited overtime was offered to help stay ahead. So I would come in at 6am and work for a couple of hours before the bulk of the team arrived. Not only did I get so much work done—no phone calls and emails—but the paycheck every two weeks was pretty nice too! The drive to work was on almost-empty highways, and I always got a great parking spot! At the end of the day, I would leave at the normal time to ensure my time with loved ones was preserved.

Even when I did not have the option of starting early and earning overtime, I still worked to leave the house at least 15 minutes earlier than needed. Few things elevate the blood pressure like being stuck in stop-and-go traffic with barely enough time to clock in before being late! On the days where I did not give myself enough of a cushion, I literally had to run to clock in on time! I had barely caught my breath before I took the first call! I remember thinking to myself: "Mental note--LEAVE EARLIER!"

By starting a few minutes early every day, we can get ahead-- ahead of our tasks and ahead of our competition. The old adage "the early bird gets the worm" still really does apply!

Keep in shape

Winston Churchill took early-morning walks prior to the busyness of his day. He said that it helped clear his mind, enabling him to better prepare and plan for the day ahead. You don't have to have a gym membership to accomplish this, although some find going to the gym to be more motivating than working out at home.

When I worked full-time for the Army National Guard, exercise was part of the morning routine before starting the day. It was easy to stay in shape because I was working out 5 days a week. When I returned to drilling status—one weekend per month and two weeks in the summer—it was more of a challenge. So I asked fit soldiers who were in the same drilling status how they maintained their exercise. Based on their advice, I added swimming 2-3 days a week in the morning before work and an abdominal workout at night that only took 15 minutes, three days a week. I found that a simple exercise plan was easier to stick with, and consistency was better than frequency. It was better to swim 2 times a week, every week, than to swim 3 times one week and none the next.

Just 15 minutes of exercise releases good hormones and inspires creativity

On top of being physically in shape, exercise has additional hidden benefits that are very important. Research has shown that just 15 minutes of exercise a day releases good hormones and engages our creative juices. See if you can fit just 15 minutes of exercise in the morning prior to starting your day. You'll experience immediate benefits and be able to more clearly organize your day simply from that habit alone. If morning exercise is not a good fit, see if you can add it after the workday. The benefits work no matter what time of the day you exercise—either as a great way to kick-start your day or a good way to wind down.

Keep positive

I like to start off the day with a practice I call the 3 Three's. This helps engage my mind in three areas that are very important to me. The first one I call "Gr-Attitudes"--three things that I'm grateful for. I like to make them fresh and new every day. To start with an attitude of gratefulness has proven to improve our state of mind, our mood, and how we interact with others.

Along with being grateful, I verbally list the three most important personal goals that I have for the day – the things that I want to accomplish for myself and my loved ones. Saying them aloud engages both my conscious and subconscious mind, providing additional incentive to cross them off my to-do list.

Lastly, I verbally express three professional goals I would like to accomplish for my career. This simple exercise while I'm headed off to work in the morning has proven to help give my mental focus a head start. The most important tasks to grow my business and take care of urgent customer needs always stay in front of me.

Keep quality first

Once I arrive at work, I like to review the tasks ahead of me by checking emails, looking at my calendar, and reviewing appointments for the day. If you like to cross things off, make a to-do list. For some people, crossing something off a physical list gives them a feel-good reward.

As we work through our list and our tasks for the day, focus on doing them with the best quality possible. Quality first, efficiency second. Webster's defines quality as a high level of value or excellence. Learn to do it the best way first—for the customer, the company and you---then find how to do it with less effort. We must be careful not to reverse that order.

Slow is smooth, and smooth is fast

When I was in military training in Texas, I'll never forget what one of the sergeants told us as we were practicing Room Clearing. This military exercise involves four soldiers, lining up outside the door of a room that may or may not have the enemy inside. The goal is to knock down the door and proceed around the outside edges of the room as quickly as possible, within seconds, to either determine if the room is safe or eliminate the enemy. The sergeant said, "Slow is smooth, and smooth is fast."

Some soldiers would rush through their practice time, and try to do it as fast as possible right away. This would result in soldiers tripping, or running into each other, or running into the door if it wasn't opened properly, or, worst of all, missing a hidden enemy as they cleared the room. The most effective way to learn the procedure was to start at the walk, then move a little bit faster, before eventually running at full speed. A smooth room clearing team is impressive to watch! The soldiers who steadily progressed, while taking their time to get the details correct, ended up doing it the best in the shortest time overall.

Keep it fresh!

Another way to be productive at work is to look for new ideas and fresh approaches. No one knows the best way to do everything all the time. Give yourself a distinct advantage by borrowing others' good ideas to help work through your to-do list more smoothly. Ask your co-workers or organized friends how they get their to-do lists done. Learn the computer systems and software better so that the simple tasks get done more easily.

When I first started working at a credit card customer service center, I recall how long it took to find answers in the system. Because I was determined to keep our customers on the phone as little as possible, I regularly asked experienced agents where to find the answers for uncommon questions. The ordinary, everyday questions became second-nature, almost instinctive, after just a few days. It was the one-off requests that I learned to look for just a short time before asking others. For the uncommon tasks, I saved notes on my computer so that I did not ask the same question a week later. While dedicated team members are happy to help, they did not like to answer the same question over and over again!

As you work through the day, focus on the progress you're making, not on the goals you have for that day. The goals are the end target you have in mind, whereas the progress is what you're actually accomplishing by crossing tasks off your to-do list. It helps us find satisfaction in what we're getting done so that we have no regrets for successfully managing our time and our priorities. After all, in a busy customer service role there is no such thing as according to plan!

In a busy day, there is no such thing as according to plan!

It is helpful to remember that providing excellent customer service and being well-organized does not require perfection. And it doesn't require having OCD! However, two common traits I found in people who were the most efficient professionals were: neat desk spaces and neatly dressed.

I found this professional principle to be consistent in every one of my career fields.

Keep it clear!

While it doesn't require being obsessive about neatness, it does take specific effort to keep space clear, especially on busy days. Always try to keep space on your desk free of documents and notes. This ensures that space is reserved for writing or making notes. Keeping space clear for note-taking is especially helpful when your day is filled with phone calls.

Another little tip is to keep the phone on your dominant side. Since I'm right-handed, I always kept the phone on the right side of my desk, and had paper handy to make quick notes. Dialing with my left hand felt unnatural and awkward; this was before I was aware of dominant-side workflow. Now it makes even more sense why it worked better for me to keep the phone and notes on the right side of my desk!

Another idea I used to create clear space was to have folders in stackable or cascading trays within easy reach; I could then organize my tasks by the papers associated with them. This kept a great deal of my desk clear while giving me easy access to information I might need at a moments' notice.

More space, faster pace

It has also been shown that the fewer reminders we have around us, the more effective they become. So try to keep sticky notes, pinned reminders and even personal decorations to a minimum. No! I am not being a party pooper! There is actual science to this! Because our brains are amazing supercomputers, they are processing everything we see. The less we physically see, the less our brains have to process. **More space, faster pace.** Too many reminders, notes & knick-knacks, and not enough clear space, slows down our processing ability and can blur things together. Ultimately, this can hinder our accuracy and efficiency.

Keep making decisions

You will probably never hear this said by any organization expert, I promise you! **I am going to encourage you to procrastinate.** That's right! Procrastinate. When I actually looked up the definition of this word, a lightbulb went off! The simple definition is: to delay or postpone action. Now that's not so bad after all, is it?! This word has gotten such a bad rap for far too long!

Do, Delay or Don't!

Because our days are so busy, we want to make sure that the most important tasks are completed every day. We want to manage our minutes well so that small, easy tasks are knocked out while saving enough time to get the top priorities done as well. How do we do that? Procrastinate! To stay ahead of our tasks I recommend one of three actions: **Do, Delay or Don't.**

Because our days are so full, I like to **Manage My Minutes** by using the **Big Rock, Small Rock, Sand** concept. In this analogy, our available time for the day is represented by an empty vase. Only a certain amount of **Big Rocks, Small Rocks** and **Sand** (To do's for the day) will all fit in the vase...but only in the correct order!

In order to fit all three items in that limited space, the items that use the most space must be placed in first—the **Big Rocks**. Our available time in the day is just like the limited space; time to complete our most important tasks must be protected. Or else the **Sand** tasks (short, simple jobs that can be done at any time & low priority) will take too much of our time, and there will be no room left--no time left--for the critical ones.

So, keeping the vase analogy in mind, the **Big Rocks** are critical tasks that must get done—the **Do's**. When the end of the day rolls around, these "to-do's" must be "done's"! **Small Rocks** are the tasks that are important, but can be moved later in the day—the **Delay's**. **Sand** tasks are the to-do's that can be fit anywhere that makes sense. Even if the **Sand** tasks do not get done today, it is acceptable to move them to the next day when more time may be available. **Sand** tasks can be either **Delay's** or **Don'ts**.

Whatever you choose, be decisive! Analysis paralysis is a real thing! And the busier our days get, the more difficult it can be to decide. On those days when it seems like one task after another keeps getting pushed out further, remember that the **Big Rocks**, the **Do's**, are the only tasks that you marked as top priority. If those **Big Rocks** are done by the end of the day, that's a win! You will always have time the following day to work on the other tasks. By realizing which tasks are critical, and which ones can wait, we give ourselves the freedom to be responsive as our busy days unfold. Remember---the goal is progress, not perfection!

Give yourself the freedom to procrastinate, and you will find that managing your time and tasks will come a little bit easier!

Your **O**rganized Order

_____

_____

_____

_____

_____

_____

_____

_____

Word Choice

"Gracious words are like a honeycomb,

Sweetness to the soul and health to the body."

Proverbs

All across the world, Ritz Carlton is famous for setting the standard for excellence in customer service. Their goal is to provide memorable, personalized experiences for every single guest. Their Leadership Center Website shared *10 Word Choices to Improve Customer Service*; they are listed, with my thoughts, below. These guidelines are consistently taught and expected of every employee, no matter what their role is, at every Ritz Carlton location.

1) **Use A Proper Greeting**

First impressions start here. "Good morning" and "Hello" are both good choices. Avoid overly-casual greetings like: "Hey there" or calling your customers "Honey" or "Dear."

2) Be Conversational but Not Overly Chummy

It's great to genuinely ask customers "How are you?" It's best not to treat customers too casually, like old friends who just walked into your house. They may find the casual approach somewhat disrespectful. Avoid common phrases like: "What's up?" or "How's it goin'?"

3) Don't Use Slang and Acronyms

Remember, we're not texting! We're having a polite and professional conversation. When we use slang or acronyms, our customers might not understand what we're saying. Customers may also feel our approach is a little too laidback or indifferent. So avoid phrases like: "You guys," "Dude," "No worries," or "BTW" or "OMG."

4) Never Start with a Negative

Rather than starting our sentence with a "No," try starting with a "Yes." A Psychology Today study found that negative words release stress chemicals in our brains and our listener's brain. The article notes "the listener will experience increased anxiety and irritability, thus undermining cooperation and trust." A healthy alternative is to say, "What we can do is ..." rather than "No."

5) Keep the "Buts" Out

The word "But" often nullifies any positive words that just preceded it! For example, if we say, "We value your business, but ..."—customers will only hear the words after the "But" and will not believe they're valued. "But" can trigger mistrust, so replace "But" with "However."

6) Choose Empathy Over Orders

Telling upset customers to "calm down" just doesn't seem to work! Try expressing compassion instead by saying, "I can see you are very upset. Let me see how I can help."

7) **Shun Phrases that are Hopeless and Helpless**

We want customers to feel that our service is trustworthy. Phrases like "There's nothing I can do" or "That's not my job," do not build trust. Our customers should never feel like they are on their own. If we can't personally help our customer, try saying, "Please allow us to find out for you" or "We will find someone who can better assist you with this."

8) **Don't Ask Customers To Solve Their Own Problems**

Customers do need to give us information, or fill out forms at times, or make phone calls in order to resolve a situation. However, when we begin by telling customers, "You need to ..." our customers can think we're making them do extra work. Along with politely asking for their help, keep the focus on the service we're delivering by saying, "So that we can help resolve this for you, can you please provide us with ...."

9) Accept Responsibility

Our customers want problems resolved—not finger pointing or excuses. They don't want to hear "It's the computer's fault" or "It's company policy." Work to keep your words focused on finding a solution rather than blaming the company, other colleagues or modern technology. Reassure them by saying, "Let's see what we can do for you!"

10) Don't Argue with Your Customer

Our customer may be right, or they may be wrong. Either way, we need to avoid arguing with them. Stating to them, "That could never happen here!" will only escalate the situation. Work to encourage them to focus on the solution we are going to provide to them.

After reading those 10 values, it is easy to see why Ritz-Carlton has set the standard in hotel customer service. Their constant concern for the customer and their focus on positive, solution-based communication ensures that guests feel welcome **and** valued.

Because this is a menu, and not a recipe, take a look at the list and see if any of them jump off the page at you. Personally, I chuckled at Number 4: never start with a negative! When giving their own rule, they broke their own rule! It's a great rule of thumb to remember when interacting with others to consciously avoid words like "No", "Never", and "Not" as the first word we say.

Number 6--Empathy: we will explore this rule in far greater detail later; it's the 6th Way in this book. Number 8-- ties in very well to the last Way we will discuss (More), and Number 10 sets the stage perfectly for what we'll talk about next – our words.

Tone

Before we talk about our words, though, it is important to start off with what is actually more important than the words we use---our tone. Is it really that big of a deal? Suppose you tell your friend, "I'm going on a trip to the Bahamas tomorrow!" And their response is, "Great." Or their reply is, "Great!" Same word, different tone! Tone absolutely makes a difference, and especially over the phone.

Studies have shown that 83% of verbal communication comes from our tone. This means that our tone is far more important than the correct words we use. On top of this, our body language affects our tone, and it carries through when we speak to people.

83% of communication comes from our tone

Research has found that the purpose of our customer's call determines the best tone for us to use. For instance, 65% of customers prefer a casual tone when working through normal transactions with us. But 78% of customers, almost 8 out of

10, reacted to having a casual tone when they had issues and needed our help.

In every interaction, we should be looking for clues:

- Does the customer use slang?

- Does the customer sound non-fluent in our language? We need to be careful with our slang.

- Does the customer sound frustrated? It is so important not to mirror their exasperated tone, as hard as that is sometimes!

    - Use an empathetic tone

        - Ensure they know we understand their concerns

        - Apologize if we're at fault

        - Reassure them that we will make things right.

Once we've developed the practice of looking for these cues, we will automatically adjust our tone to match the customer; it will become second nature, especially if our role involves a great deal of time talking with customers. We do not have to alter our personality to add sincere appreciation or concern to our conversations with customers and team members. Just add a friendly tone; it makes a huge difference!

Trust

Do the words we use build trust with our customers? Our prices and procedures, as well as the next step, need to be clearly understood so that our customers do not feel like we're trying to trick them or avoid them. Customers who can trust us will obviously do far more business with us. Trust is earned the best when we are thorough in our communication. Proactive messages are extremely helpful in avoiding misunderstanding and delays down the road. Let me share an example with you.

Our industrial automation projects often involve large capital expenditures. Depending upon the size of the purchase order, it is common practice to receive up to 50% of the total purchase before the equipment is delivered. When this is communicated with the customer before the project is officially approved, there are no surprises later. It is understandably upsetting when the accounting team tells the installation crew that their project will be held up due to funding delays! The fact that some of these projects require installation in very short time windows increases the need for proactive information. The large projects that go smoothly require a great deal of upfront communication and result in trust being established. The likelihood of earning future capital projects goes up significantly.

What *can* we do?

Tell them "Yes!"

Remember one of Ritz Carlton's values was "never start with a negative." So how can we say "Yes!" to our customers while honoring our leadership? That can be very difficult sometimes. So a great question is to always keep in mind: "What **can** we do?"

Recently, our family received our internet provider's bill, and it was significantly higher than the previous month. It was a little bit surprising to see that much of a difference, so I called them. The response I received was, "We notified you in your previous bill that the rate would be going up."

Now I don't know about you, but I don't take the time to read every page of my 6-page internet bill! I calmly informed the customer service agent that I do not read every page of my bill, and made him an offer.

"I did not see that in my previous bill," I said, "Is there any way you could adjust the bill this time to match my previous rate? I'd be willing to explore other options for the future or, if this is the best one, pay the difference on the next bill."

His response was: "The bill has printed, so there is nothing we can do." Now, I'm no genius, but I believe there was a really simple answer to this printing problem: take care of the valuable customer!

So I said, "I've been a faithfully-paying customer for years now. Is there anyone I can speak to that could help me with this?"

His response, "They'll tell you the same thing-the bill has already printed; there is nothing we can do. Is there anything else I can help you with?" Nice tone, but absolutely unwilling to help!

Needless to say, if another option becomes available for us, we will be sure to go with a new provider because of the very poor customer service we received. It was not the $20 difference; it was the fact that our business did not mean anything to them. They were not willing to explore what they could do for us. Worst of all, they were content with what they *couldn't do*.

Don't be quick with a "No."

So engage your customers, ask questions, investigate the issue. Don't be quick with a "No." After looking into it, if we do not have what the customer needs, offer a solution and a good one at that! By offering a solution, especially if we can't provide it, it proves to the customer that their best interest is most important to us. Let me share with you a personal example from an industry leader in customer service.

Because of their convenience, we regularly use Visa gift cards, purchased through Amazon, to enable our friends and loved ones to buy what they would enjoy the most. The first time I bought multiple Visa gift cards, I discovered that only two of my purchases went through. Puzzled, I contacted Amazon customer service to find out what was going on.

The agent who answered was polite and engaging. After learning what my concern was—that I could only purchase two $100 gift cards--he began to research if there was anything he could do on his end. Now Amazon has nothing to do with the policies Visa institutes for their gift cards, but I greatly appreciated his efforts to see if we had any other options. We even got disconnected during the call, and he called me right back!

Although we were ultimately limited to buying two $100 gift cards in a 48-hour period, his extra effort reinforced the value Amazon places on excellent customer service. That is one of the main reasons why our family has been Amazon Prime members for many years. Even with the recent increased cost for an Amazon Prime membership, the value of their service has been proven to us time and again.

"Is there anything else I can help you with on your to-do list?"

To-do List Offer

After helping them and making sure our customers' needs are taken care of, there is one question that is critically important for us that benefits both the customer and our company: **"Is there anything else I can help you with on your to-do list?"** This simple question can remind them of what's on their list of tasks. "Now that you mention it," I have had customers reply, "There is something else that you may be able to help me with. Do you carry this?"

This benefits the customer where they may be able to complete a couple of items on their to-do list during one phone call. It benefits our company by possibly earning an additional sale. While this may not happen on every single call, if we do not ask the question, we will never know if there was something we could help them with. So always ask!

Take care

A mental tool I use while working through customer concerns is to think of them as my family or close friends. Just like I would want to take the very best care of my loved ones, seeing customers in that same mindset helps me to more easily keep their best interest in mind.

It also enables me to think more about who the person is on the other end of the phone or on the other computer. Who am I talking to? Someone who relates with their emotions? Someone who is very social? Or someone who's very detail oriented? Or someone that's results-focused? By identifying their personality or temperament, I can take the very best care of them.

The Golden Rule or the Platinum Rule? Both!

More than once, I have observed discussions on whether the Golden Rule (Do unto others as you would have them do unto you) or the Platinum Rule (Do unto others as they would have done unto them) is best. I believe the answer is: "Both!" Initially, as we are getting introduced to each other, we start by treating the customer as we would like to be treated. As the relationship deepens over time, it should progress to treating them as they prefer to be treated.

When my wife and I were newly married, we didn't know each other nearly as well as we do now. So I would often try to help her in the way I liked to be treated: by solving the problem. Full honesty here: I was told in pre-marital counseling that I would want to fix her concern, when what she really wanted from me is to understand and identify with her concern. Countless times, I offered my advice to help solve her frustration, and, shockingly, she seemed to become more frustrated! Over many years, I have gotten much better at this, but I still catch myself using the Golden Rule in our relationship rather than the Platinum Rule. Our loyal customers appreciate it greatly when we serve them according to their preferences. It makes them feel special when they receive "Burger King Care": have it your way!

Sometimes, I have found that just listening works best, especially if customers or co-workers have issues or concerns. People are able to sort out the issues in their minds just by talking through them. My customers would thank me for my customer service which required little to no input from me at all!

If we are at fault, it is always helpful to apologize that their expectations were not met. And then promise to take action to help resolve things as best as possible. This is the ultimate way to take the very best care of our customers—own up and then step up.

Toothy Smile

When I worked in a call center for one of Chase's credit cards, I was told multiple times that I should do voiceover work. The customers said that they enjoyed listening to me talk with them, go through product details or even read disclosures! I intentionally made it a daily goal to add life, energy and enthusiasm to every phone interaction. The smile on my face impacted the tone of my voice, and customers enjoyed listening.

We do need to make sure that our tone or smile is sincere because that does come through. After all, a polite "Can't do a thing for you" is still bad! My internet bill experience—perfect example! And just to underline how important smiling during interactions is, a University of Kansas study showed that smiling during stressful situations lowered heart rate and blood pressure. Not that we have any stressful situations in the customer service world! A gentle smile is a helpful way to calmly work through stressful situations. Not because we are ignoring the customer's concern, but because we are confident that we can provide them with a solution. And who doesn't want a pleasant solution?

Top-Shelf Words

When I was in the transportation industry, I would often call my wife, very excitedly, and tell her, "I got shingles!" Why in the world would I be excited about something as terrible as shingles?! In the flatbed trucking world, a load of shingles is one of the easiest to haul. No tarps are required (yes!), they're easy to strap down, the load sits low on the trailer, and they're loaded quickly—all these things helped me to get on the road sooner with less work. Obviously, if a person did not have a background in trucking, they would think I was nuts! "He gets excited about getting shingles?!" **Every. Word. Counts.** Every word we use has impact, whether it be conscious or subconscious.

Every. Word. Counts.

On the next two pages, you'll see a short menu of what I call **Top-Shelf Words** with ideas of how to convey the same message using more positive words. I have found these phrases to be very helpful in communicating to the customer news that could be disappointing. Just like anything in this book, try them out and see if you like them!

Top-Shelf Words

- **"You owe"** upgrade to **"Our records show a balance of"**

- **"You need to"** upgrade to **"We have found what works best is"**

- **"We don't have that item in stock"** upgrade to **"We do carry _____; we expect to have inventory by _____"**

  - Add **"I will update you as soon as it arrives"**

- **"We don't sell that item"** upgrade to **"You can buy that item from _____; I will email their contact information to you."**

- **"Your PO was sent in too late"** upgrade to **"To allow timely delivery, please submit your order by....."**

- **"Your order won't be ready until...."** upgrade to **"Your order will be ready by...."**

  - Add extra time to **Under-promise and Over-deliver!**

- We can't ship the order until...." upgrade to **"Your order will ship out...."**

- We will have to replace that for you (damage) upgrade to **"The best way for us to take care of this for you will be to....."**

- **"You have to talk with Sales about pricing"** upgrade to **"Your account manager will be happy to discuss pricing with you"**

- **"We don't have the item in stock; it's on backorder"** upgrade to **"We will have stock availability on...."**

Your **W**ord Choice Order

Teamwork

"It's amazing what you can accomplish
if you do not care who gets the credit."
Harry S. Truman

No matter what the title is on our business card or desk, all of us are leaders in one form or another. We lead by what we do, not just what we say. Even the quietest person on a team still leads by what they do and what they say. Unless a person comes to work and does absolutely nothing, their contribution to the team is how they influence the team's service. And that's their leadership style.

Lead by example

The best way to lead is by example. It's one thing to tell people what they should do; it's another thing to model it, to live it. In my current account manager opportunity, I have the privilege of working for management who walk the talk, who live out and model what they expect of me. Not only does that inspire high-quality work, it underlines the core values of the organization. When I interact with our customers, I am fully convinced of the value we bring to them, on every level. Here's why this is critically important.

In one of my retail experiences, I worked for an excellent store manager. The results showed with strong sales despite being a smaller store with access to fewer customers. Our customers would make the extra effort to come to our store because of the quality of our service. The discontinuity of service excellence across the brand showed itself at the larger branch. Despite having access to more customers and space for larger inventory, that store struggled to keep invested team members and grow its base of loyal, engaged customers.

**Long-term success depends on
accountable, accessible leadership**

While adding quality team members is a large part of this recipe for service success, the most important aspect to continuity in quality comes from connected leadership that holds itself to the same standards it requires of the team. Years of work experience in a variety of career fields has proven this vital aspect to me, whether it was with small businesses or Fortune 500 corporations. Long-term success depends on accountable, accessible leadership. While all team members should strive to lead by example, it is the ones entrusted with the task of leading the organization that must be most consistent to create and support a genuine care for team members and customers.

Lend a hand

When I was working for Chase in the refinance group, it was a priority to me to hit the ground running. I saw how their morale was suffering from the high turnover, the high caseload, and the demanding job. The training took two full weeks. On all my breaks and during lunch, I was at my desk learning the processes, the systems, computer programs, and getting familiar with the paperwork. I was committed to helping the team as much as possible, as soon as possible. There was still a learning curve, of course, but, because of that intentional head start, I was able to quickly contribute to the team that was already overtasked with too many files. This boosted team morale and productivity. It also proved that I was a strong asset to the team, and my enthusiasm led to new opportunities within Chase.

A spirit of lending a hand proves to the team that it's not about me, it's about us

My career history proves that this team-first approach works. I've been recognized for the quality and energy of my work and have been rewarded with increased responsibilities, as well as opportunities to influence and train others. It's that spirit of lending a hand that proves to the team that it's not about me,   it's about us. That in itself is a huge morale booster, when others are assured that we have everyone's best interest in mind.

Basic training in the military is fundamentally designed to break down the individual focus and replace it with a group focus. In order for our unit to be effective in battle, to defeat our enemy, and to protect the health and lives of our own soldiers, it's critically essential that the team functions together. The platoons in basic training that "got it" the fastest, were the ones that succeeded the most. They quickly worked through the challenges and the stress and the difficulties together. While lives may not be in danger at the workplace, the importance of "We Versus Me" is universally appreciated everywhere we go.

Listen

Along with pitching in to lend a hand, listening respectfully to others' opinions helps create strong teams. There will always be different opinions on how to do something. The team members who are open to listening to others' ideas, whether they end up agreeing or not, show that the other team members have value. The leaders or the team members who refuse to even listen to others' ideas can cause great damage to team morale.

**Team members who are open to listening
to others' ideas show that others have value**

One customer service skill that comes from listening well to others is called active listening. This tool is essential when interacting with our customers, because it equips us well to ask the most effective questions. We can provide custom-tailored solutions for our customers, ensuring that we didn't miss anything that should've been asked. Sometimes just one question from active listening can help solve the solution for the customer. Asking one well-worded question can trigger the solution in their own minds.

Let them know they're valued

Have you ever been part of an organization where you felt valued by others on your team? What were some of the things they did that made feel welcome? One thing I do is send short, encouraging emails to team members to tell them the great job they're doing, or how much of a help they are to me, or how well they handled a difficult situation. It only takes a minute or two to type up an email or share it with them face to face. It can impact others far more than you may realize.

Timely words of encouragement can change a person's life

When I worked as a counselor at a summer camp, I'll never forget what the camp director said to me at the end of a grueling eight-week camp season. I was in charge of anywhere from eight to ten 10-year-old boys every week. You can imagine how much energy it took to take good care of them! So, on week eight, I was feeling pretty drained. The camp director came up to my table, and said: "John, at the beginning of the summer, I wasn't sure how good of a counselor you would be for us. But I can honestly say, that you're one of the best counselors we've got. You've done a good job." I suddenly didn't feel that tired anymore. Those words meant so much to me and only took a minute or two of his time. I will remember his encouragement the rest of my life. Timely words of encouragement can change a person's life and certainly brighten their day!

Along with helping our team members feel appreciated, we can also help them improve their processes, how they do their job. The phrase, "Fix the process, not the blame" applies here! We are not pointing fingers or passing the blame along to somebody else. First-class customer service organizations foster an environment of positive accountability, where continuous improvement is really the most important thing. An engaged team member only needs to be reminded of these things. They will work hard to improve them.

Leverage

Remember the definition of synergy? Webster's defines it as: "the increased effectiveness that results when two or more people or businesses work together." I know it's a little wordy, but hear me out!

A team will always accomplish more than one person ever can

A team will always be able to accomplish more than one person ever can. No matter how good Michael Jordan was as a basketball player, he would never be able to take on five guys at once! Synergy takes energy, which is singular, and multiplies it. Our singular energies are merged into a collective force that accomplishes even more. It's not addition; we're talking about multiplication, squared! My apologies if this example triggered some rough days in algebra! I say that, because it did for me!

Ritz Carlton gives every employee at their hotels the freedom to provide a solution to take care of their guests, up to $2000 each day. For bean counters like me, don't focus on the $2000---look at the spirit behind this value! Every single employee, from room service to maître d', is empowered to provide solutions for their guests. You may be thinking to yourself, "Gee, that'd be great, but it would never happen where I work!" That's okay! Money is not the only requirement to provide that same level of service. We will always have customers who need solutions, so the opportunity to creatively work together to provide them, no matter what our title is, is available to all of us. It's what sets world-class team members apart. A problem-solving spirit, coupled with an organization that embraces extraordinary service, results in a customer service powerhouse that sets the standard for every other company in their industry. Like Ritz-Carlton.

Along with being empowered to provide solutions, creativity and ideas should be welcomed within your team. This is common practice at companies that have first-class service, that are always rated near the top by consumer surveys. After all, we will get better results from our collective efforts when those ideas come from within the team. And ultimately, celebrations mean far more when our team overcomes challenges together.

Leadership

For those of us specifically in leadership positions, it's important to keep our team clued into the big picture, the 30,000 foot view. This does tie into the **Why** of what we do. As leaders, casting a vision involves inspiration and direction, providing the team with goals to shoot for and a clear path to get there.

Leaders who are most effective in the business world have a coaching mindset rather than a manager mindset. There are specific company roles called managers, so I'm not referring to those career fields. What I'm referring to is our approach to mentoring others. Coaching is about mentoring, collaboration, and working alongside, whereas management often has the elements of instruction, discipline and pushing beyond comfort zones. Ultimately, it's the spirit and purpose behind the instruction that differentiates coaching versus managing.

When I was a section sergeant in Iraq, we provided 24-hour radar protection of American bases in 12-hour shifts. A young soldier was in training with a younger sergeant on the night shift. My supervisor said that the young man was having a hard time learning the procedures. His nervousness only created greater friction between him and the young shift leader. My supervisor asked if I would be willing to move to the night shift to help mentor the soldier. I quickly agreed.

Seek to mentor others rather than manage them.
You will see greater productivity with less effort.

Within a week, the soldier had settled into his role, and our teamwork made for a smooth, calm shift. My goal to mentor, encourage and coach worked more effectively than adding more structure, discipline and oversight. Many people have difficulties in their backgrounds that can trigger subconscious reactions to leadership that feels overbearing. Seek to mentor others rather than manage them; you will see greater productivity with less effort. And they will thank you for it!

Nordstrom is known across the U.S. and Canada for its exceptional customer service. Their team members go to whatever length is necessary to take care of their customers. In one instance, a customer returned tires to the store, and

they credited the customer for them. Here's the kicker---
Nordstrom doesn't even carry tires!

"Ask your top people what they need,
because they have the answers."
Bruce Nordstrom

This doesn't happen by accident; this comes from one of the core values of Nordstrom's leadership. Bruce Nordstrom said, "Ask your top people what they need, because they have the answers." Nordstrom employees are empowered and entrusted to take the very best care of their customers. In companies like Amazon, American Express and Nordstrom, there is a consistent value on entrusting their people with innovation while pursuing the company's goals. It's not surprising that that these companies are consistently top-rated for their customer service efforts.

Look for top talent

Another aspect of leadership is adding quality people to the team. I'm glad to see that it's becoming more common to make hiring decisions with a greater emphasis on a person's talents and personality than their resume. I've seen the following quote attributed to both Sir Richard Branson, the founder of Virgin, and Nordstrom, "Hire the smile, train the skill." No matter who came up with it first, it is not surprising that both Nordstrom and Virgin excel at customer service! Genuine kindness, caring for others, an optimistic attitude, a focus on the team and a desire for excellence and integrity as non-negotiables – these are all qualities you will not find on a resume. You will often find them in the person sitting across from you who is considered to be "too old" or "too experienced" or "too young."

Three years ago, I was told, "John, you're too old to begin a new career; stay with what you have." Two career steps later, and I have the best job of my whole life! Why? Because the owner recognized these qualities in me and provided our family with a life-changing opportunity. My resume did not strongly support the open position, yet he chose to hire me based on his read of my personal character and abilities. I am incredibly blessed with how much we have been given because of his trust in the value I could add to the team.

Hire self-motivated people, who are also kind; it's well worth the extra time to find them!

So hire self-motivated people, who are also kind; it's well worth the extra time to find them! After all, you're developing brand ambassadors, people who are going to be putting forward your company's image to your customers. That should not be lightly entrusted to anyone. We should make sure that, as much as possible, the team members that we add contribute to the positive synergy, the company goals, and the absolute essential of taking care of our customers.

Once we've identified candidates who have agreed to join the team, it is essential for leadership to recognize, reward, and retain those people. Retention not only requires attractive pay, but there are two elements that are even more important than the compensation. A CareerBuilder study showed that the top three reasons why employees stay with their company, or leave for another, are:

- Recognition for their work (or the lack of it!)
- Work/life balance
- Compensation

I can personally vouch for the fact that I have had some well-paying jobs that we're not satisfying and lacked a positive work environment. The pay was not worth the stress, the lack of purpose, and the lack of genuine kindness. On the other hand, I am blessed to be part of an organization that values all three of those. The difference is incredibly important.

Excellent customer service does not happen by accident. And it's not because companies get lucky with who they hire. It is a very intentional pursuit on every level of the organization.

Learning

While this last item may not seem like a teamwork tool, learning our customers should be a team priority. Here's how we break this down. Contact resolution is a technical term that means the fewer times a customer changes hands within our company to get to a solution, the better. Built into this metric is next-issue avoidance. What good does it do to quickly provide them an answer if another customer is going to have the same issue later on?

The focus must be on a quality resolution as opposed to the time needed to provide that solution.

First contact resolution, without keeping the same issue from happening again, will result in a **higher** call volume that can be totally avoided. Providing a solution without identifying the root cause of it, means that we are not learning our customers or their needs or their processes. We're simply filling orders. Industry leaders in customer service do not just fill orders. Their frontline personnel are freed to deliver smooth, effortless solutions and share those solutions throughout the team.

We will touch more on the effortless part of customer service that is absolutely critical in the 7th Way. For now, remember that the team focus must be on a quality resolution as opposed to the time needed to provide that solution. There are metrics that are constantly monitored within the customer service world about handling time, about first contact resolution. But those are only the tip of the iceberg. To get rid of the iceberg, you've got to dive deep. This involves learning about our customers, their points of pain, their needs, and their processes. Even more importantly, the invaluable solutions must be communicated to the entire team, or future customers are going to experience the same frustration.

When we're responding to our customers, make sure that we are replying to them in their preferred method of communication. This is huge! As simple as this may seem, this can be a real stress-saver for our customers. There are some people who love to talk to us on the phone, and then there are others that appreciate the convenience of answering an email when they are free. Make sure that if there are multiple team members serving the same customer that there is some way to identify their preferred method of communication. This creates a seamless transfer regardless of who serves the customer; their preferences are being followed. Ritz Carlton is one of the companies that does a fantastic job of this, and it is common in the companies that strive to provide world-class customer service.

Why are customers calling us?

Most importantly, the question we really should be asking is "Why are our customers calling?" Do they want to or do they have to? Why do they have to call? What is causing them to contact us in the first place? And what is causing them to contact us again? If their preference is to call us on the phone for every need, then first contact resolution or calls from the same number on a repetitive basis do not mean that we're failing. As a matter of fact, it means that the phone-friendly customers are contacting us the way they like the best. And that's a good thing! So frequency of calls does not necessarily mean that our customers are not being well served. That can be a misleading metric. However, if the same person is calling, about the same issue, and it's not being resolved, then we are in danger of losing them and all the people that learn about their frustrating experience.

All of us would enjoy being part of a positive, energetic, enthusiastic work environment. If that's not possible for you at this time, it's still an excellent practice to begin focusing on being the team member that everyone loves to work with. For all we know, the best career of our lives could be the next career step! By practicing now, we are establishing ourselves as an excellent team member; we are preparing ourselves for that role we would love to have. And that may be just around the corner! Resolve to be that team member who is a proven asset, who adds value to their team, and who takes the very best care of their customers. You will be invaluable everywhere you go!

Your Teamwork Order

_____

_____

_____

_____

_____

_____

_____

_____

Humor

"A day without laughter is a day wasted."
Charlie Chaplin

I might date myself a little bit by talking about this old saying! If someone was said to be "good humored", it meant they had a pleasant personality. Having a sense of humor, no matter what form it takes, is critically important to keeping morale high, especially during stressful, heavy workloads in the customer service world. I remember when I worked in a retreat center in an outdoor job. Our leader would refer to rain as "liquid sunshine!" None of us liked working out in that cold, damp, fall weather, but you can imagine how much harder it would be to work together and serve our customers well if the leader's attitude was negative about the rain. It's setting that kind of an example, no matter what our role is, that can dramatically affect our team.

"But, John," you may be thinking to yourself, "I am not a bubbly, outgoing person." That's okay! A workplace needs multiple personalities to create holistic synergy—too much of the same personality can actually cause friction. Sameness is not the goal; maintaining a positive work environment that cherishes excellent customer service is.

I love my job! One of the main reasons is the excellent care our customer service team provides to our customers. There are all different kinds of personalities and skill sets, but the one common quality among them is that they engage our customers. Some have a bubbly personality, while others have a quieter, more serious demeanor. I have seen all of them smile, share a laugh or ask how our customers' days are going. It's not about the personality; it's about the person.

Think about it---how many ingenious, innovative leaders in history would be considered as fun-loving? Not many! But their steady, unwavering commitment to their goals enabled them to accomplish much. Every team needs good-humored, faithful people who keep calm and carry on! So as we work through this recipe ingredient, remember that the idea is more about an attractive attitude than a peppy personality.

Smile!

When I came into my role with Chase refinance, the turnover was high, the stress levels were high, the amount of work each processor had was much higher than what was ideal. So I determined to be a day-brightener at work. I wanted to help encourage people, and one way to do that is to have a sense of humor. There are some that have a dry sense of humor or a sarcastic sense of humor. As long as it's towards themselves or something outside of the workplace, sarcastic humor can be something that helps lighten the mood. Some people tell jokes once in a while, or some like puns, while others tell humorous stories. Whatever your style is, it should be used to help your team function even better. Studies have shown that laughter and humor boost creativity, energy & productivity, help manage stress, and build stronger connections within the team.

Q-TIP: Quit Taking It Personally!

Having good humor is not necessarily telling jokes all the time. It can also include the ability to be resilient, to do something called **Q-TIP: Quit Taking It Personally**. In the customer service world, this ability to translate a good humor into a strength is very important. When we are able to **Quit Taking It Personally**, our good humor helps to keep us focused, to be faithful to the team, and consistently work to improve the process. Most importantly, it enables us to provide fresh experiences for every single customer.

When we had high call volumes at a credit card call center, it was absolutely essential that I treated the very next caller like I had never spoken to them before. My conversation with them had nothing to do with the last call---whether it was an upbeat, positive, easy conversation or a difficult, challenging call with stressful issues.

One of the key reasons why I was consistently a top performer in customer satisfaction ratings was because I treated every person as a fresh new experience. The last call was the last call. I use the same approach today, even though my role does not require as much phone time. **This phone call, this email, this interaction, this meeting, this appointment---it's all new for them, it's all new for me. That's Q-TIP in a nut shell.** Our good humor enables us to do that well!

Smiling is a central part of how our good humor translates into our service to our customers. Brian Tracy, a top sales trainer, credits smiling with a few key benefits.

- It builds others' esteems

- It creates confidence in ourselves and with our customers

- It encourages positive attitudes in others

- It stimulates a spirit of cooperation

Success stories

Another thing that can be helpful to brighten our days or to lighten the stress is to keep success stories in mind about how we have helped people. This underlines the fact that we are good at what we do. And this can really help on those difficult days, enabling us to keep a good humor, to keep a good attitude, to remain positive by remembering that we do take excellent care of our customers. The success stories give us a feel-good satisfaction. They boost morale, especially when we share them with others on the team. They reinforce the value that we bring to our customers. When I share with customers how we have helped others in the same situation, it has inspired a greater confidence in doing business with us.

One great way to publicly share outstanding customer service is on the company website. After gathering feedback from existing, loyal customers, create a Testimonials or Customer Reviews tab on your website. A Forbes article shared 7 benefits to regularly updating your testimonials:

- **Client loyalty**—faithful clients appreciate being asked for feedback and mentioned by name

- **Referral dress rehearsal**—provides talking points when interacting with prospective customers

- **Natural language from customers**—versus advertising writing that can blend in with other companies' marketing

- **Learning opportunities**—not all feedback will be positive, providing ways to improve service

- **Staff appreciation**—who doesn't like being mentioned by name for excellent customer service?!

- **Shareability**—easily shared across social media

- **SEO**—feedback can provide great ideas for blog posts, which boost your website's SEO score

Snippets of fun

Another tool I've used to help keep a good humor is to save short YouTube or Facebook favorites. Even during a short break, it's helpful to pull up a funny YouTube clip or a Facebook post--something that makes us chuckle or smile.

Those little things in the course of a day can help keep that good humor, that positive attitude, so that when we interact with customers, we are engaged and enthusiastic.

Laughter IS the best medicine!

The old saying, "Laughter is the best medicine" is so true! After a busy day of customer service, set aside some time to listen to music or watch a favorite comedian or surf social media or browse YouTube. Whichever form you choose, I strongly encourage you to find media that brings a smile to your face or laughter to your heart. The benefits are proven scientifically!

The Mayo Clinic showed laughter had both short-term and long-term health benefits. Laughing after a tough day at work lightens our mental load, stimulates our hearts, lungs & muscles, and releases feel-good hormones. Strong laughter actually mimics a stressful situation by raising our pulse rate and blood pressure but in connection with something positive. The end result is a good, relaxed feeling. It also improves circulation and muscle relaxation. Those are just the short-term benefits!

In the long run, intentionally adding laughter to our daily to-do list improves our immune system, relieves pain, increases personal satisfaction, and improves our mood. Talk about a game changer! No matter what kind of entertainment you like best, add humor to your daily routine. It will become easier to find the humor in our everyday lives, improving our life and the lives of those around us.

Taking care of our customers should be fun! Who would you rather have taking care of your order---Ben Stein in *Ferris Bueller's Day Off* ("Bueller, Bueller") or Jack Black in *School of Rock*? An enthusiastic person can take an ordinary experience and transform it into an extra-ordinary one!

> **An enthusiastic person can take an ordinary experience and transform it into an extra-ordinary one!**

When I have the opportunity to take care of people, there's a smile on my face, energy in my voice and gratitude in my words. Do you love to take care of people? Excellent customer service starts with genuine enthusiasm from people who love what they do. Refreshing customer service is hard to find and greatly appreciated by customers hungry for businesses who enjoy serving them. So have a blast when you serve your customers, and watch your business explode!

Share it!

It is important for our team to share things that are humorous; don't keep Day Brighteners to yourself! If it's funny to you, it is very likely to be funny to someone else on your team. After all, we want to be the team member who others enjoy being around, who feed positive energy. We want that good humor, that **Q-TIP** ability, to be contagious rather than the things that take energy away.

A positive determination to endure until we overcome will always get us closer to our goals.

Imagine if I stated in the introduction: "I'm positive you're going to like this book!" While that may have seemed slightly arrogant to say, hear me out! An intentionally positive attitude is not seeing life through rose-colored glasses nor the idea that everything is always wonderful. It really boils down to a numbers game--the more positive effort I pour into my life, the more positive results I will achieve. It's that simple! Especially during the challenges, a positive determination to endure until we find a solution will always get us closer to our goal of providing world-class service. A positive mindset encourages fresh creativity, win/win collaboration, upbeat communication, and the unflinching drive to never, ever give up—all of which are must-have's in the demanding world of customer service.

Put yourself in others' shoes--who would you rather share life experiences with? Be a positive influence in your life and the lives of those around you. Just like in math, one positive action on top of another adds up to a grand total. Better than numbers on a page, our cumulative, positive actions lead to an abundant life. So start adding on the positive side today. You literally have everything to gain!

Simple

I have a fairly active imagination. That can get me in trouble sometimes! And here's how this applies in our role of serving our customers: it's critically important that we work to reduce or avoid drama. I'll share a couple of personal examples with you.

A co-worker and I were growing our company's presence on social media. One of the platforms that we used often was LinkedIn. My job was to create a post on certain products or services to be posted on a weekly basis. The first time I sent a draft to him, there was no reply. So I thought, "Sweet! A perfect first effort!" What actually posted, a couple of days later, was nothing like what I had written--it was much shorter, didn't have all the words, heck, the message wasn't even what I wanted! I was tempted to be pretty upset about that! I had put a lot of work into this! It looked nothing like what I had written! But I wisely decided to connect with him first and find out what was going on. It turns out that the post had to have a maximum of 700 characters, not words, characters. This included spaces, punctuation, the web links, and the words. So I had to learn the art of writing what I wanted to say in far fewer words in order to get the message out within the character limit.

Another example that often happens in my life involves my family. Suppose I'm expecting a call from my wife at a certain time. She doesn't call. Minutes go by, then hours. I start to get a little concerned! Is she in a ditch somewhere? Is the car dead on the side of the road? No, turns out she was having a great time visiting with her friend, and the minutes passed a lot faster then she realized. Especially in the cell phone era, almost everybody has one. If my wife did need something, she would be sure to call. It was my wild imagination that was blowing something up to a much bigger deal when she was

just fine.

In our customer service roles, it's critically important that we ask the right questions and find out what's really going on. Because e-mails or voicemails or messages can be so short of details, our imaginations can run wild! Ask the questions to find out how we can help them. Most often, I found that the issue(s) and the solution(s) were far simpler than what my fertile imagination came up with!

Your **H**umor Order

_____

_____

_____

_____

_____

_____

_____

_____

Empathy

"I believe that empathy is the most essential quality of civilization."
Roger Ebert

At the very beginning, we noted that there were two tools that are absolutely essential to providing world-class customer service. Just like a basic meal at a restaurant includes a drink and the main course, excellent customer service requires, at a minimum, two vital aspects.

The first key, like the main course of the meal, is a fresh understanding of **W**inning. The second must-have, like your beverage choice, is better **human** service. A Genesys survey of more than 9000 customers found that 40% of them said this was most important to them. As a matter of fact, it was twice as important as the next closest answer of the survey! Every industry leader in customer service strives to make their service feel more human and less scripted.

Have you ever found yourself thinking that the support you just got over the phone, or by email, or in person was excellent because it felt human, like you were understood, like you were talking to a person? Not someone just reading a script or just going through the steps they had been trained to do, but someone who genuinely cared about you, about what you needed, about how they could help you?

> **"Empathy is about standing in someone else's shoes, feeling with his or her heart, seeing with his or her eyes. Not only is empathy hard to outsource and automate, but it makes the world a better place."**
>
> **Daniel Pink**

That refreshing experience comes from something that's very real and absolutely essential: Empathy, the ability to put ourselves in others' shoes. We have to work to understand our customers' worlds. This should not be too hard, after all, we're customers as well! We know how we like to be served when we purchase a product or service.

Because it's our job to take care of customers, it's important to not let our work become so routine that we lose the personal aspect. It's critically important for customers to want to do more and more business with us. Especially in the difficult interactions, where issues have to be resolved or a customer's expectations were not met, we have to think like the customer in order to take the best care of them.

It is possible to apologize without blaming anyone, by apologizing that their expectations were not met. That's really what we want to do in the first place, to exceed their expectations. However, apologies can be just saying "Sorry", and that's as far as it goes. I've experienced this (our Internet bill experience), and it's very frustrating! Apologies are meant to show that we understand how they feel, and that we're genuinely disappointed that their expectations were not met. We acknowledge their concern, then engage our problem-solving process. Genuine empathy, that brings a solution with it, encourages people to like us and trust us.

People like me!

One of my supervisors in the credit card service industry did a fantastic job with his team members and his customers using the same skill: listening. He listened, identified the concern by repeating it back, and helped them work through what they needed. This is an invaluable skill, and it comes from a genuine concern for the well-being of others. This is what builds up our trust "bank account" with our customers.

Think of it this way: taking the best care of our customers is like putting money in the bank. The more we follow through with what we say we will do, the more engaging and enthusiastic and human we are as we interact with them, the more trust we build up with them—the more money (trust) we deposit into our bank account (customer loyalty). The time is going to come where their expectations won't be met, and that loyalty account will suffer a large withdrawal. Because we have deposited so much good faith with them, our trust account will keep them with us rather than looking elsewhere.

Team members accomplish more with people they like, and customers buy more from people and businesses they like. Here are **7 Ways** that have been proven to attract and keep engaged customers. I call them the **7 Be's**!

- **Be Thankful!** Sincere thanks shows our appreciation

- **Be Trustworthy!** When we do what we say we will do, trust is added to our Loyalty Bank Account

- **Be Credible!** When the facts we share are proven to be true, more trust is deposited

- **Be Honest!** Especially when we do not know the answer, saying "I do not know, so I will research this and have an answer to you no later than tomorrow morning" adds to our trust account. Making up information can bankrupt our Loyalty Account instantly!

- **Be Knowledgeable!** Take the time to learn as much as possible about your products/services. Confident service will encourage customers to contact us first when they have an urgent need

- **Be Genuine!** Be yourself AND be professional. Add your personal flair to your service to be fresh and interesting, while keeping your communication above board

- **Be Humble!** Be quick to credit others and the customer. "We" is always better than "Me"

Personal connection

Whether it be over the phone or in person, do our customers connect with us? I know that in today's social media age, it can be a challenge to connect to the point that people actually engage with us. I don't mean connect where we are just another connection, one of thousands, on a social media site. Do people feel like they know us, and, more importantly, do they feel like we know them? It's those emotional attachments that are actual connections that grow our base of loyal, highly-satisfied customers.

Here are some ideas. Try to figure out what the customer is doing that you like—their unique name or fun email address.

Or maybe they are placing a large order or a cutting-edge product; thank them for their business and compliment them on their innovative addition. Use grateful phrases like:

- "I see that you have been with us for 5 years; that's a long time!"

- "I appreciate your patience"

- "Thank you for being so positive"

- "Your business means a great deal to us!"

- "Thank you for taking the time to speak with me today"

Another simple, but often overlooked, way to connect is to ask for their name and use it, within reason!, throughout the conversation. People remember the beginning and the end of the conversation most clearly, so use their name at the beginning, somewhere in the middle of your conversation, and when you're wrapping things up.

Passion for excellence

So what fuels the effort to grow our base of connected, loyal customers? Our passion and enthusiasm! In my current role supporting industrial automation solutions, a specialist and I were having lunch before going to an appointment. We are both very passionate about providing industry-leading products and quality solutions to our customers' processes. We were talking about how important it is to provide the best product with the best service to grow long-term, win-win relationships. One of the ladies at the table behind us said, "Excuse me! I don't know what you're sellin', but I'd buy it!" Our enthusiasm was so engaging that she felt compelled to tell us! Her job had nothing to do with automation, and she wasn't going to be a customer of ours. It's that kind of enthusiasm for what we do, and how we do it, that attracts people; they feel like they just have to be a part of it!

Pleasure to do business with us!

There are some people who greatly appreciate gratitude; saying "thank you" means the world to them. There are a great number of studies that prove saying "thank you" and "please"--common courtesies—are very important to our customers. They should enjoy doing business with us, because we show them how deeply we appreciate their choice to do business with us. In today's global, online marketplace, they could go to any number of companies that provide the same thing, and perhaps for a lower price. But, because they enjoy doing business with us and we clearly appreciate them, they think of us first. An unusual aspect of the pleasure of doing business with us is actually best proven when things do not go as expected. Until problems arise, the quality of our service is unproven. Any company can take care of processing an order correctly. That's not when excellent customer service is proven. It's proven when expectations aren't met, when they didn't receive the item they wanted, or the product is broken, or the service was not what they expected, or the food didn't taste the way they expected, etc. So here is how industry leaders prove the value of their service:

- They identify the issue, making sure they clearly understand the problem

    - They don't just take care of the issue with a knee-jerk reaction

        - They want to fully understand how expectations weren't met so that they can not only resolve it, but work to prevent it from happening again

- They promise specific action and then follow through

    - In a very specific time frame

- If this issue has come up before, they're diligent to address it internally so that other customers or, even worse!, the exact same customer, do not experience the same thing again

Preferences

One of the reasons Ritz Carlton is so good at what they do is because they make sure that every customer experience is tailored to that customer. They do this by gathering and saving every single preference of every guest. Then they give all their employees access to that information. So no matter which hotel the customer stays at, in any part of the world, they can see what they prefer for: dining, room service, entertainment, how they prefer to be addressed, and special events in their lives.

In your current role, you may not have the ability to capture those specific details; the ones who can definitely should! Especially those in sales! With how many people we serve, it's very important that we have easy access to what makes our customer unique. Another way to do this is to ask for their feedback, with questions like:

- "How are we meeting your needs?"

- "How can we improve our service to you?"

This helps them feel valued as a customer because were asking for their opinion. But it also can reveal to us what is very important to them. Invaluable information like this can be used by our sales, marketing and customer service teams to best serve those customers.

Prevent burnout

How would you feel if you helped grow a company to a multi-million dollar industry only to have it cheated away from you? A close friend of mine helped grow a transportation company from a start-up to a multi-million dollar business. And he was cheated out of his 50% share of the success. He was faced with two options: be bitter and angry the rest of his life, or make the best of what was in front of him. He chose the second option because he told me, "John, I could be bitter the rest of my life but that would only hurt me and the ones I love. So I chose to let it go, and focus on the life that was ahead of me, not the life I could've had." Interestingly enough, the man who swindled him out of his fair share has a family that has fallen apart, poor health and no close friendships. Richard, on the other hand, is one of the kindest, gentlest, most patient men I know; he taught me an invaluable lesson about letting go.

Burnout is one of the most common reasons for turnover in the customer service world. Empathy is an essential quality so that we can let go. We need to be patient, understanding, and refuse to allow others' stress or busy lives to affect the quality of our lives and our service. Remember **Q-TIP--Quit Taking It Personally**? People who genuinely employ empathy in their interactions with the customers have greater resilience and are able to work under high-pressure situations without burning out, day in and day out. They gladly take ownership of their actions and respond well to constructive criticism, because continuous improvement is their ongoing commitment. This enables them to concentrate on demanding tasks for several hours, all with high-quality results.

Your very best work, everywhere you work, will always work out for the best of others and yourself.

It wasn't luck or just who I was or my temperament or my faith or my intelligence or my military background that brought repeated successes in demanding customer service roles. I used all of those ingredients to whip up a daily masterpiece of tasty customer service—everyone who tasted it wanted more! You can cook up the same yummy dish; start with a genuine concern for others. Your very best work, everywhere you work, will always work out for the best of others and yourself.

Put ourselves in others' shoes

Empathy is not just about feeling bad for others. If that's the extent of our concern for others--simply feeling bad about what's going on in their lives--we will never be able to emotionally engage or connect with them. The ability to work to understand their world is an invaluable skill that enabled me to be a consistent top performer in taking care of my customers. This is one tool that has to be a personal value to implement. It cannot be magically added by reading books or starting a course or by occasional training. It has to get to an individual level where we commit ourselves to the well-being of others. When we do that, it translates through all of our interactions. I work to make sure that my customers genuinely know, beyond the shadow of a doubt, that I have their best interest at heart. And that's why they like to do business with me.

People are hungry to be valued as human customers. Empathy enables us to look past the product or service and engage the person. Strengthen your ability to empathize, and you will experience higher and higher customer satisfaction, an increase in sales and a growing number of referrals from highly-satisfied customers. Oh, and you'll sleep well at night, too!

Your **E**mpathy Order

More Than Expected

"Always deliver more than expected."
Larry Page, co-founder of Google

We touched on the 7th Way (**More**) briefly in the 1st Way (**Winning**). We saw that **Who** we are taking care of is a great motivator as to **Why** we do what we do. We don't want our customers to come away with less than what they expected or even exactly what they expected. So here's what it takes to go above and beyond.

Exceeding expectations

When I worked in retail, I was the assistant manager for a retail store in the Northern KY/Cincinnati International Airport. Only airline employees had access to the store. The store manager was one of the most enjoyable leaders I have ever served with. He made excellent customer service such a critical value that airline employees would go out of their way to come to our store. We were located in a smaller airport, so it was harder for them to get to us. Their flights were more often routed through the busier airport with the larger store. They made the extra effort to buy from our store as often as possible because of our exceptional customer service. The reason for their loyalty and referred business came from what I call the Positive Ripple Effect.

The Positive Ripple Effect---it's worth it!

When you throw a rock into a pond, the ripples radiate from close to where the rock landed and, depending on the size of the rock, can ultimately expand across the whole pond. Studies have shown that the negative experiences of our customers spread faster and stronger--like throwing a boulder in the pond--than the positive experiences--like throwing a pebble. Both create ripples, but the negative experiences reach farther and move faster with harsh, disruptive ripples.

Think about it---which do you hear more often?   The great customer service someone received or the terrible shopping experience they had?   The negative experiences are shared more often.   How much more?   According to a ZenDesk survey, 54% of consumers are likely to share negative experiences, while only 33% share positive ones.   And, to magnify the potential impact, 6 out of 10 people, of all age groups, are likely to share their experiences, positive or negative, on social media.

The Positive Ripple Effect takes a lot more effort to create an attractive environment and sustain it.   It does pay off! Going the extra mile in customer service----our hard work, our values, our leadership, our sincere appreciation for their business----encourages customers to come back to us again.

This atmosphere of positive customer experiences has to be supported by creativity, initiative, and the freedom to act. It should result in win-win situations that are good for the customers and good for our company.   No reasonable customer expects to get everything for free; they expect to pay. They also really want to enjoy doing business with us. The most important way to help them enjoy that, is to surpass, to go beyond, their expectations.

"Do our customers come away with more?
Is that a top priority for us?"

So how do we do that, how do we become industry leaders in the service we provide? It first starts by honestly asking ourselves, "Do our customers come away with more? And is that a top priority for us?" We certainly don't want them to get less than they were expecting in their experience with us, but we don't want them to get exactly what they expected either! After all, would you make it a priority to return to a place that provided service that was no better than anyone else?! Especially if you could get the product for the same price somewhere else? I wouldn't! Why should our customers?!

It doesn't have to be a lower price or free stuff that keeps them coming back to us. As a matter fact, a lot of items that we sold to airline employees could be purchased somewhere else for less. They appreciated our customer service, our support, and our guarantees so much that they thoroughly enjoyed the entire shopping experience in our store.

Nordstrom has that effect perfected! Their customers love to shop at Nordstrom, because they are greatly valued. They know absolutely that Nordstrom will take the very best care of them, and they are willing to pay more for that kind of service. Our personal efforts to exceed our customers' expectations mean far more than anything they physically receive. The goods or services they receive from us are not what's most important to them. **The fact that they are valued by us is what's most important**. If this principle were not true, the lowest price would be chosen in every single purchase across the world. We know this is simply not the case. Let me share an example from the industrial world.

In the manufacturing world, an integrator is a third-party company that installs new equipment and trains the engineering team of the factory to use it. Because the engineers at most manufacturers are very busy, integrators are invaluable partners who help automate and improve processes by completing major projects. Having an integrator who does quality work is critical.

A major automotive manufacturer chose an integrator with the lowest price and the least amount of experience. Not only did the integrator fall behind in the installation timeline, he didn't even show up to complete it! With time running out, the manufacturer hired the top-quality integrator who had bid on the project, but was not chosen due to the higher price tag. They not only completed the project on time but also with excellent quality. It's no wonder that 95% of this integrator's business is with existing customers or referrals! Quality does matter, and their customers always come away with expectations exceeded!

Eventful approach

Every time a little girl goes to Disneyland, she is expecting to be treated like a princess. When you stop to think about how many cute little princesses go through Disneyland in a day, let alone a year!, it would be easy for the Disney employees to treat every little girl the same. But one of Disney's core values is to make sure that every guest feels special, that every cast member goes above and beyond to exceed guests' expectations.

The Eventful Approach:
Turn the ordinary into extra-ordinary!

I call this the Eventful Approach – our normal, everyday transactions are treated like special events because of our customers. I know, I know! You might sell office supplies, valves, toilet plungers or light switches--ordinary products. None of these are fun, none of these have "Party!" written all over them! We have to remember that "Good enough" is the enemy of "Great!" We want our customers to have a great experience with us. It requires taking the everyday, ordinary transaction and transforming it into extra – ordinary. So here are key principles that help our service stand out from the crowd.

Everyone's concern

For industry leaders in customer service, providing customers with the very best care is everyone's concern. Are your customers' concerns heard and are they helped? It's not just enough to know their issues, it is far more important that the issues are heard **and** addressed promptly with a smile. The background on my laptop has a saying I found on LinkedIn: **"Your smile is your logo, your personality is your business card, how you leave others feeling after an experience with you is your trademark."** Companies that provide world-class customer service have that priority as the one of their trademarks. Taking the very best care of the customers is everyone's concern---from the CEO to the person greeting guests in the lobby. Everyone in the organization is valued, resulting in all of their customers being valued.

The manager of the retail store at the beginning of this chapter trained every staff member to make sure a guest was greeted when they entered the store. A friendly "Hello!" with a smile made everyone from a pilot to a baggage handler feel welcome and appreciated. It was one of the ways that our store set the standard for customer service across the company.

Ensure results

One of the best ways to ensure results is to under-promise and over- deliver. In the manufacturing world, products are engineered with margin in mind. The design of the tool must have enough capacity to overcome the challenges of the workplace: dust, contamination, wear, operator error, power loss, etc. I've always made it a priority to promise what I know I can do, within my own power, within my own abilities. When it involves others' time frames and inputs, I am careful to include additional time to give us all extra time so that our customers receive what they need by the time we promised.

And if I'm not able to meet that timeframe, I am diligent to make sure they are updated with where we are in the process, and how soon we expect to deliver. Either way, a solution or an update is provided in a timely matter when we said we would have it to them. It is far, far better to quote two days and deliver in a day and a half, than state it will take two days and arrive in two days and one hour.

Effortless

Studies have shown that customer efforts feel twice as difficult to the customer as the energy they actually use. If we can lessen our customers' efforts, we will be able to proactively prevent future issues. Not only that, but the same study showed that 96% of high effort experiences were directly connected to customer disloyalty, our customers going somewhere else. On the other hand, when customer effort was lessened, 94% of customers would buy again. 94%! Add 94% to your current sales, and see what that does for your bottom line! Why does this work? Because the customers feel valued, because we made it as simple as possible for them to buy with us, their response is: "Let's do that again!"

**When customer effort is lessened,
94% of customers will buy from us again!**

A Forrester survey found that 41% of customers expect a support response in six hours or less. I would submit to you that in today's global, fast-paced environment, six hours is often too long. In six hours, a customer can go online and find innumerable options at the same price or lower. So two key questions to ask before offering a solution is, "What is the customer's timeframe to receive their order?" and "How soon would they like to have a quote or estimate?" In some cases, we may not be able to accommodate the preferred delivery timeframe, but our customers will know that it advance and plan accordingly.

Escape the Blame Game!

Because of hard well-water, our family purchased a water softening system. Loved it! A few months after we bought the system, it seemed to be cycling far more than we expected. We were told that our system came with a warranty, so we scheduled a technician to come out and evaluate the system to make sure it was running properly. My wife really enjoyed interacting with the technician--he did a great job and made sure our system was working to its fullest.

A few days later, we received a bill for $90! We were not expecting this charge, so I called the company. The manager answered the phone, and, unlike our internet bill experience, completely restored our confidence in them by both waiving the charge and then offering to get with his team to see if they could come up with a way to help our system cycle less. Ultimately, this resulted in them offering a solution that would require an additional investment from us. Because I knew they had our best interest at heart, the investment to help the system run even better because of our hard water, was a no-brainer. Not only did the manager not blame anyone within his team, he also provided a proactive solution. When we escape the blame game, we provide solutions rather than identify more problems.

Similar to Kyle's excellent response, industry leaders in customer service thank customers for alerting them to concerns or issues. They view these challenges as opportunities to improve their processes, rather than complaints. After all, we do want loyal, highly-satisfied customers!

Engage

In today's competitive credit card marketplace, it's fascinating that American Express charges their customers for the privilege of using their card! But there is a reason for that! I can personally attest to the excellence of their customer service. Like all industry leaders in first-class customer service, American Express does not provide this by accident. They have a consistent approach to engage every customer.

When they engage the customer, they are careful to match the pace, tone and personality of the person they're speaking to. This ensures that the transaction, whether it be a normal one or working through issues, that the customer's preferences are followed.

Secondly, they work to identify the customer's needs rather than just taking care of what they're asking for. The root issue is not necessarily the thing they ask for first, so well-thought, well-worded questions are needed.

Thirdly, after fully understanding the customer's needs, viable options are offered. But reasonable solutions alone do not take care of what the customer needs. As a matter fact, good ideas without action will give them a good reason to look somewhere else! There are two more steps that must be implemented for engagement to work.

Next, they inform the customer with the details and the benefits included in the solution they are providing. Whether this comes at a cost to the customer or not, the more details and benefits that are mentioned, the value of the solution becomes more important whether there is a cost attached or not.

And lastly, they prove commitment by doing what they say they will do, in the time they say they will do it. **Make sure to follow through!** It doesn't matter how good our product or service is, if we do not follow through on what we say we will do, our customers cannot trust us, and they will go somewhere else.

Your **M**ore Than Expected Order

_____

_____

_____

_____

_____

_____

_____

Conclusion

With how busy you are, thank you very much for choosing to spend time with me! Please remember these 7 things to get the most out of this menu:

- **It's a menu, not a recipe!** Refresh your definition of **W**inning and add a healthy helping of **E**mpathy—those two Ways are must-haves! Add the other ingredients that work well for you!

- **Write down very specific goals**, personal and professional. You will achieve at least 30% more of them!

- Take notes as you connect with fresh ideas and post them where you can regularly see them.
  Be What You See!

- Please send us your feedback so that we can post it on our website! Your emails with questions and suggestions are welcome and much encouraged. The **7 Ways** approach is a living resource; continuous improvement is the goal. Your input is highly valued!

- Host a **7 Ways in 77 Minutes** workshop for your team! All attendees will receive a copy of *WOW Your Customers! 7 Ways to World-Class Service* and an engaging, interactive session to bring the **7 Ways** to life!

- Please share this menu with others! If the **7 Ways** have been a help to you, please encourage your friends, co-workers and customers to get a copy for themselves! But only after you register, for free, on our website and receive a unique promo code! You will receive **unlimited Thank You Bonuses** every time your code is used. So register today, and share the **7 Ways**!

- Stay tuned for a life-changing "menu" coming next year, going deep on winning more. I promise you—it will change your life like it did for me!

Bibliography

Gelman, Andrew. 2013. *"The Average American Knows How Many People?";* https://www.nytimes.com/2013/02/19/science/the-average-american-knows-how-many-people.html

Collins, Jim. 2001. *"Good to Great";* New York: Harper Collins.

Kolodny, Lora. 2010. *"Study: 82% Of U.S. Consumers Bail on Brands after Bad Customer Service",*
https://techcrunch.com/2010/10/13/customer-service-rightnow/

DiJulius III, John R. 2008. *"What's The Secret to Providing a World-Class Customer Experience";* New York: John Wiley & Sons.
p. 5

Sorenson, Susan & Adkins, Amy. 2014. *"Why Customer Engagement Matters So Much Now";*
http://news.gallup.com/businessjournal/172637/why-customer-engagement-matters.aspx

Gallo, Amy. 2014. *"The Value of Keeping the Right Customers";* https://hbr.org/2014/10/the-value-of-keeping-the-right-customers

Koslow, Sally. 2001. *"How Exercise Makes You More Creative";* http://www.health.com/health/article/0,,20412092,00.html

Morin, Amy. 2015. *"7 Scientifically Proven Benefits of Gratitude";* https://www.psychologytoday.com/us/blog/what-mentally-strong-people-dont-do/201504/7-scientifically-proven-benefits-gratitude

http://ritzcarltonleadershipcenter.com/2014/04/10-word-choices-that-improve-customer-service/

Newberg, Andrew, M.D. & Waldman, Mark. 2012. *"The Most Dangerous Word in the World";* https://www.psychologytoday.com/us/blog/words-can-change-your-brain/201207/the-most-dangerous-word-in-the-world

Brehm, Kayla. 2014. *"Customer Service Skills: Tone";* www.help.com/blog, 10/23/14

Kraft, Tara & Pressman, Sarah. 2012. *"Grin and Bear It! Smiling Facilitates Stress Recovery"*; www.psychologicalscience.org

http://ritzcarltonleadershipcenter.com/2013/08/440/

Stark, Peter. 2014. *"How to Build a Culture Rich in Creativity and Innovation";* https://peterstark.com/culture-creativity-innovation/

Ewoldt, John. 2015. *"Did Someone Really Return a Set of Tires to Nordstrom?";* http://www.startribune.com/did-someone-really-return-a-set-of-tires-to-nordstrom/330414071/

Spector, Robert & McCarthy, Patrick. 2012. *"The Nordstrom Way to Customer Service Excellence."* New York: John Wiley & Sons. p. 20

Hunt, Ryan. 2014. *"One in Five Workers Plan to Change Jobs in 2014, According to CareerBuilder Survey"*; http://www.careerbuilder.com/share/aboutus/pressreleasesdetail, January 9, 2014

Martinuzzi, Bruna. 2014. *"Laugh Track: How Humor Can Enhance Employee Productivity"*; www.americanexpress.com/us/small-business/openforum, 11/10/14

Tracy, Brian. 2017. *"How a Smile Can Affect Self-Esteem: Building Healthy Relationships with a Positive Attitude"*; https://www.briantracy.com/blog, 2017

Rajan, Vikram. 2017. *"Top Seven Overlooked Benefits of Testimonials"*; https://www.forbes.com/sites/forbescoachescouncil/2017/06/1 5/top-seven-overlooked-benefits-of-testimonials/

Mayo Clinic Staff. 2016. *"Stress Relief from Laughter? It's No Joke";* https://www.mayoclinic.org/healthy-lifestyle/stress-management/in-depth/stress-relief/

Chen, Michelle. 2018. *"Customer Service: Its Importance and Value"*; www.woveon.com/blog, 4/30/18

Dimensional Research. 2013. *"Bad Customer Service Interactions More Likely to be Shared than Good Ones"*; https://www.marketingcharts.com/digital-28628

Kober, Jeff & Jones, Mark. 2018. *"Disney's Four Keys to a Great Guest Experience"*; http://worldclassbenchmarking.com/disneys-four-keys-to-a-great-guest-experience/

Dixon, Matthew. 2013. *"The Effortless Experience"*. New York: The Penguin Group

Leggett, Kate. 2016. *"Your Customers Don't Want to Call You for Support"*; https://go.forrester.com/blogs, 3/3/16

Made in the USA
Lexington, KY
29 October 2019